My Life in a Nutshell

My Life in a Nutshell

Cindy Pimentel

Edited by: Teresa M. Shafer

Sherechita Publications 2013

Sherechita Publications
Sparks, Nevada
www.teresamshafer.com

ISBN: 1463520735
EAN-13: 978-1463520731
Cover art is an original piece by Teresa M. Shafer

Contents

Dedicated to my mom Christine
and my niece Raquel,
Thank You for always believing in me, even when I
didn't believe in myself!

Forward

Cindy Pimentel is a young lady that is filled with strong and powerful emotions. It is not an exaggeration to say that her young life has been simply bursting with a myriad of trials and tribulations. And to her family's great relief she has not been taken by the fires that have consumed others. She utilizes the modern equivalent of a pen and paper to discharge her anger, resentment, fear, love and hope onto the blank pages on her computer screen. This practice has once again proved that the written word still serves as an apt release for pent up emotions and helps to keep a person sane in an insane world.

Ms. Pimentel has poured out her emotions onto the pages here and the resulting poems are heart wrenching, soulful, illuminating and memorable. She, as they say, let it all hang out and held nothing back. Sometimes her words are disturbing and certainly not for the faint of heart. But they are honest and sincere and they were at least at the time truthful.

This expose of Miss Pimentel's life and soul document only part of her journey. As with all people she has more road to travel emotionally as well has physically. It is my sincerest hope that she continues to document her emotional journey and share those thoughts with us in the future. But for now we must be satisfied with the offering that she shares with us here in *My Life in a Nutshell*. Not that anyone shall be left empty after reading only one of her poems, but we can be greedy and ask for more.

Teresa M. Shafer

Deep Emotions

Please Hear my Screams!

I'm screaming.

The screams get louder and longer with every breath
but still nobody can hear them.
WHY?
Why can't you hear my screams?
If you would just take the time to listen maybe you would
understand how hurt and angry I am;
How I feel lost and mixed up inside.
I'm weak yet I stand strong,
not because I am but because I have to
for you, for her, her him, for them.
Yet everyday tears pour, but still nobody sees.
I'm drowning inside from the tears I cry.
Hope is all I have
but that too is becoming small.
I try to hold on to the hope I have left,
but each day that passes a little slips away along with
my sanity.

CAN YOU HEAR MY SCREAMS NOW?

How much longer is it going to take?
I can't live like this
I just can't.
The pain is taking over my body

My mind is going in circles
I'm overwhelmed
I try to make it stop but I can't.
These emotions and thoughts are getting more powerful.
Why is this happening to me?

It was never supposed to be like this.
I have to be strong but I'm losing my mind.

Can you hear my screams now?
Can you?
Can you hear them?
I need you to listen
I need you to hear my screams before it's too late.
Please
Oh please

PLEASE HEAR MY SCREAMS BEFORE IT'S TOO LATE!

Have You?

Have you ever felt as if you were not where you're supposed to be?

That you're spinning in circles, circles that are supposed to take you up but instead are bringing you down.

You can't stop it no matter how hard you try and all you can do is just sit back and cry.

You think to yourself nobody will ever get it 'cause they have never lived one minute in your shoes.

You want it all to stop 'cause you know you're going to end up hitting bottom,

and you know when you get there it is going to scare you out of your mind.....

Have you?

A Day of Crying

Have you ever had a day where everything makes you cry?
You look at something in the world and tears come to your eyes.
And when you go and dry them off it seems they're wet all over again,
because you choose to face the world but don't know where to begin.

Have you ever looked at him and thought to yourself... why?
Wondering why he can't love you the way that you love him,
and when you find out the reason why it breaks your heart in two;
because you know if it weren't for her he would love you too.

Have you ever had a dream ever since you were little,
to have a husband, a couple of kids, the perfect family?
But the older you grow the further the dream gets
so you stop trying and face the reality it will always be a dream.

Have you ever had a friend who's tried to make you see?
She tells you you'll be happy again just give it a little time.
But you don't believe her, happiness has come and passed.
So all you do is sit back wishing you were gone.

Have you ever had a day where everything makes you cry?
You look at something in the world and tears come to our eyes
And when you go and dry them off it seems they're wet all over again
because you choose to face the world but don't know where to begin.

I'm Lost

I'm lost,

I'm lost between mine, yours and ours.
I'm lost between good times and bad times,
between should haves and could haves,
ups and downs, lefts and rights,
between here and there,
between can and can't.

I'm lost between whys and why not's,
yes no and maybes,
between truths and lies
between fake and real.

I'm lost between love and lust,
between wills and won'ts.
I'm lost between reality and what's in my mind.

I'm Lost!

Deep in my Heart

I wish people knew how I felt deep in my heart,
How much it hurts when they call me ugly and fat.
How it feels to hear things, hurtful things,
things that would usually make people cry.
Instead I pretend, put a smile on my face
and laugh it off as if it doesn't hurt but it does!
I'm tired of pretending to be happy because I'm not.
I wish people knew how I felt deep in my heart.
In the bathroom is where I can let out my pain,
I can talk to the person in there and she just listens.
She cries with me and feels my pain,
she understands.
She does not judge me.
But I cannot live in the bathroom.
So again I put on my fake smile
as I walk into the world.
I just wish people knew
how I felt deep down in my heart!

Boyfriends

Things I Hate

I hate it.

I hate all of it.

I hate life, feelings, memories and thoughts.

I hate the way nobody gets along,

The way people say things they don't really mean.

I hate the fact everyone judges people before meeting them.

Most of all I hate myself.

I hate myself for thinking there could ever be

anything more between Chip and me.

I hate myself for thinking about him all day non-stop.

I hate it.

I hate it.

I hate it.

But I love him so much!

Fears

My heart begins to pound
and my mind begins to race.

My body turns cold and pale
as I began to pace.

Now butterflies are in my stomach
There's a ringing in my ear.

I focus on your face
as my thoughts turn into fears.

My voice is suddenly muted
as tears fill up my eyes.

I'm battling all these emotions
yet there's nothing but silent cries.

I try and think of something else
but only you is what I see,
as I began to wonder
are you really meant for me?

Kiss by kiss I know the answer
and my fears just melt away.

You're the one, the only one
it was meant to be this way!

I Love the Way....

I love the way
you look at me
and the way
you make me feel.

I love the way
you touch me
and the fact
that you are real.

I love the way
you wear your clothes
and the way
you fall asleep.

I love the way
you laugh
and how
you make my
knees go weak.

I love the way
you tickle me
and everything
you say.

I love that
you are you
in every single way!

I Need to Know

the Truth

I need to know the truth
on how you really feel
before I get caught up
in feelings that are real.

I don't want to be hurt again
by a man that I care for
to have him say those special words
then leave my heart there sore.

So tell me now will you be there
to cheer me when I'm sad
to be the man, the guy I trust
the boyfriend I never had?

About You!

Sleeping and
weeping and
waiting all day.

Hoping and
wanting and
needing you back.

Thinking and
praying and
wishing you're ok.

Loving and
caring and
wondering about you.

Excepting and
living and
meaning to see you.

Taking and
talking and
sharing my feelings.

How Do I?

How do I tell the one I love truly how I feel?
To let him really know what I mean so I can began to heal.
I don't know if there is a way to make him understand.
But I will try my hardest the beginnings where I'll begin.
I remember the first day I met you, you told me your favorite color was blue,
we played cards in your living room, that's when I realized I liked you.
You told me you liked my sister so I tried to back away.
It really hurt to know that you liked her, but still I decided to stay.
The next few days we only talked a few days after that.
Then we met your friend named Chris, on the couch is where he sat.
The next few weeks the five of us we hung out more and more,
but every time you looked at her it made my heart so sore.
The night us four went to the fair I had a feeling that was new,
because it was the very first time I'd told you I liked you.
Does July 20th ring a bell for you for any reason?
It does to me I remember it well it was the perfect season.
It was the day of our first kiss, I never will forget it.
I want to thank my sister because she's the one who said it.
It was because of a truth or dare question, that all my dreams come true.
It was the night I realized you had liked me too.
The point of all of this really should be clear.
You made me so happy I cried those happy tears, but honestly,
I want you to know my love for you is still there
and when you need someone to talk to
Remember I'll always be there!

Dark Thoughts

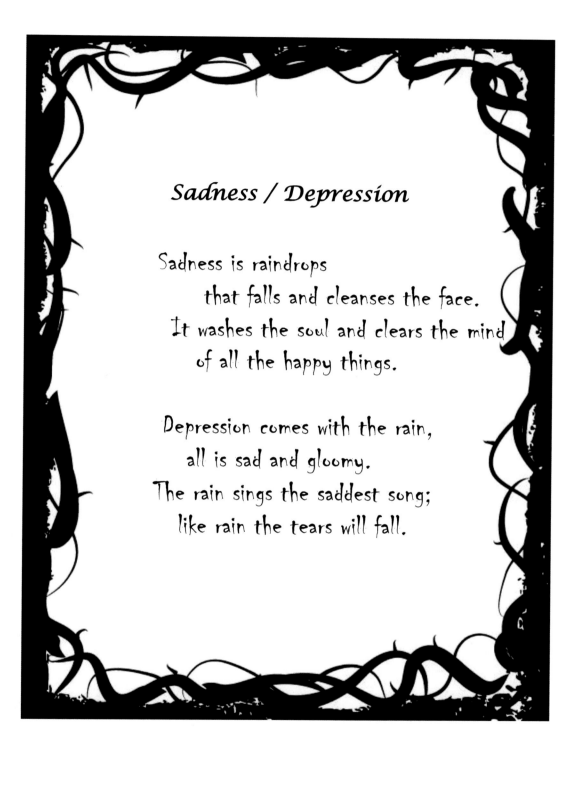

Sadness / Depression

Sadness is raindrops
       that falls and cleanses the face.
It washes the soul and clears the mind
     of all the happy things.

Depression comes with the rain,
     all is sad and gloomy.
The rain sings the saddest song;
     like rain the tears will fall.

I Want to Die

I don't want to be here.
      I don't want to stay.
I want to die.
      I can't live this way.
The feelings I feel,
      Aren't good anymore.
I hate everything;
      There's nothing to live for.
My head has stopped thinking,
      My heart has grown cold.
I'm dying inside,
      My body's full of mold.
I've made my decision,
      My mind is made up.
I go into the bathroom
      With a razor to cut.
The blade is now
      Pushed against my skin.
With one swift move
      I can feel it within.
My body is numb,
      Blood all over me and the floor.
I look over and see
      somebody walked through the door.
They run to me fast
      I just close my eyes.
Not feeling a thing
      I am paralyzed.

Calling Back

After a long day of drama
        She comes home and just sits
Thinking, hoping, wanting,
        All the bad thoughts to leave her head
Afraid they'll over power her
        She calls up a friend for help
RING, RING, RING
        No answer
She sits again
        Trying to overpower her mind with good thoughts
Bunny rabbits,
        Her boyfriend,
Family;
        but it's not helping
It makes her think of more problems
        What to do?
Suicide on her mind
        She grabs a knife
Holding it in her hand
        Ready to cut.
The phone rings
        She stops
It's her friend
        Now crying, she puts down the knife
        Realizing it's not the answer!

Death

Death
Cloudy, scary
Hurting, grieving, losing
An easy way out
Suicide

Death Events

Someone,
Unsatisfied
In life
Causing
Inappropriate
Death
Events

What to do

She's sad and depressed
not knowing what to do now
she decides to die.

Suicide

Someone,
Scared and confused
Searching for
Something to
Stop the
Sadness.

I am a Person with Thoughts on Suicide

I am a person with thoughts on suicide.
I wonder why people commit suicide.
I hear people talk about it.
I see the pain it leaves behind.
I want people to see there are other options.

I am a person with thoughts on suicide.
I pretend not to hear when people talk about it.
I feel out of place when suicide is the subject.
I try and touch people's hearts when they want to die.
I cry for them every night before I go to bed.

I am a person with thoughts on suicide.
I understand nobody's life is perfect.
I say to them "it will get better just give it some time".
I dream one day people won't use it as an option.
I try to help as much as I can.
I hope they will realize suicide is not the answer.
I am a person with thoughts on suicide.

Family

I'm from......

I'm from the good, bad, happy and the sad.

I'm from living with my mom and never seeing my dad.

I'm from going to school every day and hearing what they have to say.

I'm from seeing my family break apart and not being able to mend their hearts.

I'm from being shy and still reaching for the sky.

I'm from the good, bad, happy and the sad.

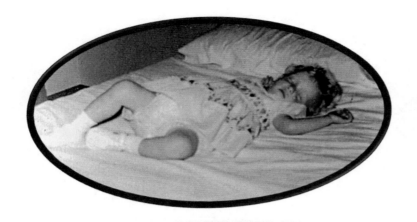

People's Differences

Aunt Loma
    sometimes outspoken
        with the things that she says speaking her mind
        without using her head.

She's pretty high maintenance
    yet lazy too
        always has something
        fancy and new.

Her sister's much different
    with nothing to say
        she'll sit there in silence until things are ok.

She's quiet and calm
    and very plain looking
        but she picks up and clean she's very hard working.

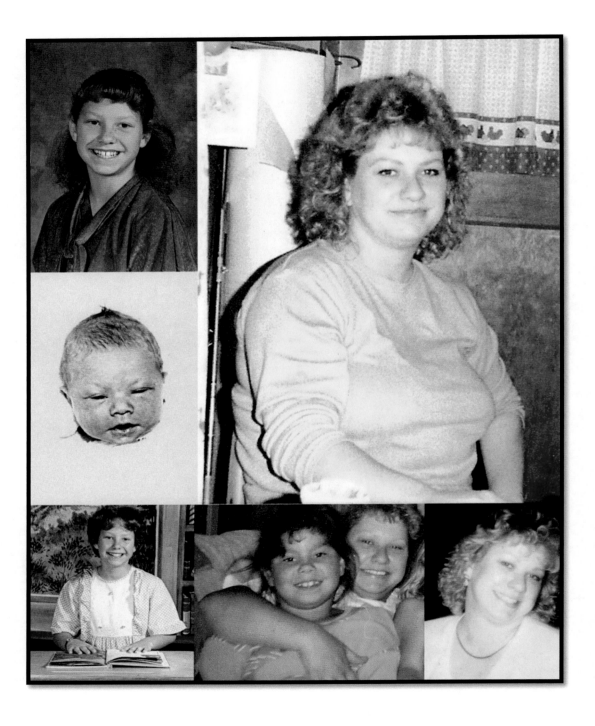

My Sister

I don't know how to do things now that you're gone
I still needed your help
I needed your help with mom.

Every time she was sick
and I didn't know how to help her
I came to you.
You always knew the answer.
You always made it better.

When I couldn't handle things anymore;
when things seemed overwhelming,
I'd come talk to you and you would tell me,
we would get through this together.

I learned a lot from you Ann;
things I'll never forget,
like how to make bows for Christmas.

You are my older sister,
and with every day that passes without you
I want you to know....
I love you and I miss you!

Summer of 2003

That summer was the worst one yet, all we did was get upset.
We had the cops called twice on us; all that did was make a bigger fuss.
My sister ended up in West Hills for taking way to many pills.
My oldest sister really sucks, all she does is beat her kids and do drugs.
My brother though, is the mean one; he won't let anyone have any fun.
He beats on us if we do wrong, even if we stick out our tongue.
My dad doesn't even know I'm here, but he's the one everyone fears.
My mother does not know what to do, so she is left with the blues.
Me I'm left in the middle, hoping to survive these little riddles.
Living each and every day, praying my life will not stay this way!

I'm From T.V.'s and Radio's

I'm from beds and dressers in my room from flower pots next to the broom TV sets and radios, this is how my life goes.

I'm from photo albums under my bed
from ties and clips on my head cats and dogs in the yard no my life is not hard.

I'm from "out mits vou" and
from "listen while I talk to you"
baklava and ice cream I hope this poem hasn't made you scream.

I'm from brothers and sisters
family and friends let's hope you liked this poem because this is where it ends

Introspection

Lasting Impressions

Saddened feeling
Broken hearts
Painful tears
It's just the start.

Hurtful hands
Piercing cries
Rude remarks
and severed ties.

Silent screams
Shattered faces
Ugly words
Horrible places.

Dreadful games
Blank expressions
Twisted emotions
With lasting impressions!

Drinking's Wrong

The nights that I got drunk some feelings came over me.
The feelings were real and strong they made me really see.
It made me see that drinking's wrong and makes you do things that are
bad.

They say it makes you happy,
but inside it made me sad.
I got touched in places that shouldn't have been touched.
And taken advantage of they told me that they wanted me and what they
felt was love.

But is it love when I say no?
Still they touch me and ask for more.
Why is it that you hurt the ones
you say that you care for?
Now I know it was all a lie
they were just playing there games.

But it's hard for me to be mad
because I might have done the same.
I know now what they did was wrong
and I should have stopped it right then and there.
But I didn't, I made a mistake
but I wish I would have dared.

Waterfalls

Waterfall are nice
they sound relaxing and calm
whooshing splitter splat

Wind

The wind comes
with the roar of a lion
it races threw the city
and blows things around
until the sun goes down again
and then it starts to calm.

Paper

A piece of paper
sits on the table all alone
with nothing by it.

Birds

Birds fly in all skies
their feathers glide with the wind
here, there, high and low.

The Mysteries of Life

The mysteries of life never to be explained we sometimes choose to ignore them but the questions stay the same.

Like.... how and when will the world end and where will we go from there?

Will I ever find true love with a person that really cares?

Why is it that my whole family
seems to be so crazy, and why when

I'm at school learning things my brain seems to turn hazy?

Will I ever succeed in life and be what I want to be, or will I be like the rest of my family and never really be free.

The mysteries of life never to be explained we'll always want to know the answers but only the questions will remain.

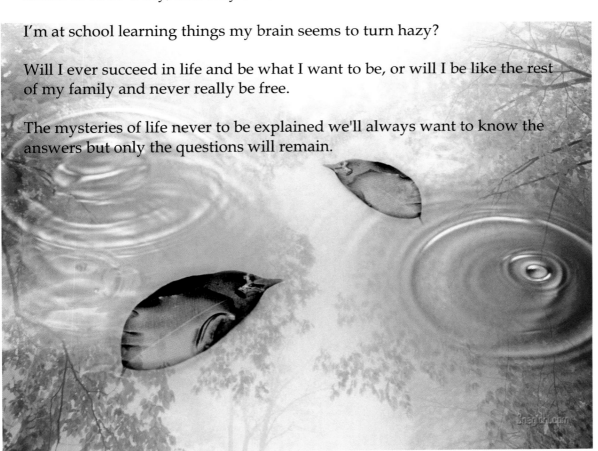

Stars

One by one I count them laying there at night
One by one I wish on them to make the world go right.

Laying there I see them they sparkle and they shine
Laying there I wish one could be just mine.

One by one they tell a story on great things that could be
One by one I listen to the advice their giving me.

Laying there I realize all the little things
Laying there I realize life's not what it seems.

One by one I tell people stars are dreams come true
One by one they hear me and their dreams they do pursue.

Made in the USA
Monee, IL
10 July 2021